Acknowledgements

The publishers would like to thank the following sources for permission to reproduce illustrations:
E.T. ARCHIVE: pp.28, 29, 83; MARY EVANS PICTURE LIBRARY: pp.14, 80; FINE ART PHOTOGRAPHIC LIBRARY: pp.6–7, 8, 11, 17, 18, 20, 22, 25, 26, 31, 34, 36, 39, 40, 41, 43, 44, 46, 49, 51, 52, 55T, 58, 60, 62B, 63, 65, 68, 71, 72, 75, 77, 78, 81, 85, 86, 89, 92, 94, 98, 99, 101, 102, 105, 109

The publishers also wish to acknowledge the following sources for quotations:
IRISH PROVERBS by Laurence Flanagan (Gill & Macmillan, Dublin);
DUBLIN TENEMENT LIFE, AN ORAL HISTORY by Kevin C. Kearns (Gill & Macmillan, Dublin);
THE LADY POETS, AN ANTHOLOGY selected by Joan Forman (Jarrold Publishing, Norwich);
LIKE A FISH NEEDS A BICYCLE AND OVER 3,000 QUOTATIONS BY AND ABOUT WOMEN edited by Anne Stibbs (Bloomsbury Publishing, London);
PILLARS OF THE HOUSE, AN ANTHOLOGY OF VERSE BY IRISH WOMEN FROM 1690 TO THE PRESENT edited by A.A. Kelly (Wolfhound Press, Dublin);
THE COMPLETE LETTERS OF LADY MARY WORTLEY MONTAGU edited by R. Halsband (Clarendon Press, London);
LOVE'S WITNESS, FIVE CENTURIES OF LOVE POETRY BY WOMEN compiled by Jill Hollis (Robinson, London);
JOURNAL TO STELLA by Jonathan Swift (J.M. Dent & Sons, London);
AUTOBIOGRAPHY AND CORRESPONDENCE OF MARY GRANVILLE, MRS DELANY edited by Lady Llanover;
ENQUIRE WITHIN UPON EVERYTHING (Madgwick, Houlston, London);
POEMS by Denis Florence MacCarthy (M.H. Gill, Dublin);
VOICES ON THE WIND, WOMEN POETS OF THE CELTIC TWILIGHT edited by Eilís Ní Dhuibhne (New Island Books, Dublin);
FAVOURITE POEMS WE LEARNED IN SCHOOL edited by Thomas F. Walsh (Mercier Press, Cork);
BETWEEN INNOCENCE AND PEACE FAVOURITE POEMS OF IRELAND edited by Brendan Kennelly (Mercier Press, Cork);
LETTERS AND ESSAYS, MORAL AND MISCELLANEOUS by M. Hays; JOURNAL OF A LADY OF FASHION by Marguerite, Countess of Blessington;
RETROSPECTIONS OF DOROTHEA HERBERT by Dorothea Herbert;
A SOLDIER'S WIFE, AN AUTOBIOGRAPHY by Lady Elizabeth Butler;
CASTLE RACKRENT by Maria Edgeworth (J.M. Dent & Sons, London);
THE ABSENTEE by Maria Edgeworth (J.M. Dent & Sons, London);
A LITTLE IRISH GIRL by J.M. Callwell;
FLORENCE MACARTHY by Lady Morgan;
RE-ECHOES by Frances Power Cobbe;
THE IRISH COUNTRY HOUSE, A SOCIAL HISTORY by Peter Somerville-Large (Sinclair Stevenson, London);
ANCIENT LEGENDS OF IRELAND by Lady Jane Francesca Wilde (Speranza);
CONSTANCE MARKIEVICZ by A. Haverty (Pandora Press, London)

KATHARINE TYNAN's work reprinted by permission of the literary executors of Pamela Hinkson

Edited by FLEUR ROBERTSON
Designed by SARAH STANLEY AND HEATHER BLAGDON
Picture Research by FELICITY COX
Production by RUTH ARTHUR, KAREN STAFF, NEIL RANDLES
Director of Production GERALD HUGHES

This edition published in 1997 by CLB
Distributed in the U.S.A. by BHB International, Inc.
30 Edison Drive, Wayne, New Jersey 07470

Ref 16285 An Irish Woman's Book of Days
This selection
© 1997 Waverley 1770, Godalming, Surrey
All rights reserved.
Printed and bound in Singapore

ISBN 1 85833 801 8

PREVIOUS PAGE: *Dreaming*, CHECA Y SANZ, ULPIANO (1860–1916)

A GIFT FOR

· ·

FROM

· ·

CLB

An Irish Woman's Book of Days

INSPIRATION

AND

CELEBRATION

An Irish Woman's

JANUARY

*'And what can the thousands upon
thousands do for me? Hearts, you
know, Lady Anne, are to be won
only by radiant eyes.'*

MARIA EDGEWORTH

1

1800 *Birth of Maria Edgeworth, Irish author best known for* Castle Rackrent
1800 *Birth of Gretta Bowen, Irish artist*

2

Songs of our land, ye are with us forever

FRANCES BROWNE

3

1925 *Birth of Maureen Potter, Irish actress and comedienne*

4

'Where the red wine-cup floweth, there art thou!'

CAROLINE NORTON

5

1826 *Separate Irish currency abolished and replaced by sterling*

6

1800 *Birth of Anna Maria Hall, Irish novelist, travel writer and philanthropist*
1794 *Birth of Frances Ball (Mother Mary Theresa), Irish founder of the Sisters of Loreto*

7

'And all the young ladies … said … that to be sure a love match was the only thing for happiness where the parties could any way afford it.'

from *Castle Rackrent*, MARIA EDGEWORTH

Here, my dear Aunt, I was interrupted in a manner that will surprise you as much as it surprised me, by the coming in of Monsieur Edelcrantz, a Swedish gentleman, whom we have mentioned to you, of superior understanding and mild manners; he came to offer me his hand and heart!!

MARIA EDGEWORTH
writing to her aunt,
Paris, 1802. She was
to remain unmarried.

8

1779 Birth of Julia Glover, Irish actress
1926 Birth of Iris Kellett, Irish international showjumper

9

1594 Trinity College Dublin, Ireland's first university, opens its gates to students

---

10

You'll live during the year, for we were just talking of you
TRADITIONAL PROVERB

11

*1935 American Amelia Earhart becomes the first woman to make a solo flight
across the Pacific Ocean*

*The grey mornings I well
remember,
The grey mountains new-
waked from slumber,
The grey dews on the trees
and hedges,
And in grey distance the grey
sea's edges.*

from The Grey Mornings
KATHARINE TYNAN

12

1930 Birth of Jennifer Johnston, Irish author
1887 Birth of Máire O'Neill (Molly Allgood) Irish actress and fiancée of J.M. Synge

---

13

Home was home then and the people friendly
KATHARINE TYNAN

14

A good heart never went to hell
IRISH PROVERB

---

*I'm Irish, you know, it
all comes of that',
Norah would say modestly
when complimented on her
fertility of invention. There
was nothing indeed of
which she was so proud as
her Irish name and her
Irish descent, although she
herself had never set foot in
Ireland …*

*from
A Little Irish Girl*
J.M. CALLWELL

A Labour of Love, WILLIAM M. HAY (FL. 1852–1881)

JANUARY

❧ **15** ❧

1860 *Birth of Eleanor Hull, Irish author, folklorist and Celtic scholar*

❧ **16** ❧

1816 *Birth of Frances Browne, Irish poet and children's storyteller*

❧ **17** ❧

First woman: Whenever I'm down in the dumps, I get myself another hat.
Second woman: I always wondered where you found them.

ANON.

❖ 18 ❖

1822 *Theatre Royal in Hawkins Street, Dublin, opens*

❖ 19 ❖

1787 *Birth of Mary Aikenhead, founder of the Irish Sisters of Charity and St Vincent's Hospital, Dublin*

❖ 20 ❖

1926 *Birth of Patricia Neal, Oscar-winning American film actress*
1908 *Opening of the Municipal Gallery of Modern Art, later named for Hugh Lane, Parnell Square, Dublin*

❖ 21 ❖

1894 *Birth of Theresa Davy, Irish playwright*
1861 *Birth of Katharine Tynan, Irish poet and journalist*

❖ THE IRISH MANNER ❖

I wish you could see the sort of comfort all these families have in one another, you would then think of a large family as a blessing. I must admire the Irish manner of bringing up children, for in all the families I have happened to know there seems the most perfect ease and confidence, and except for their attention to each other you would never find out which were fathers and mothers and which were daughters … even the Duke of Leinster, where there is a good deal of state, I could not help admiring the great grown up girls stealing an opportunity when they thought the company did not mind them to go to their father and mother with an appearance of affection that did them good. I will adopt this comfortable fashion if I can with my own children in spite of the vulgarity of it, for I am convinced familiarity with one's children is looked upon in that light by a great many of the English.

LADY CAROLINE DAWSON from Ireland to her sister in London, 1776

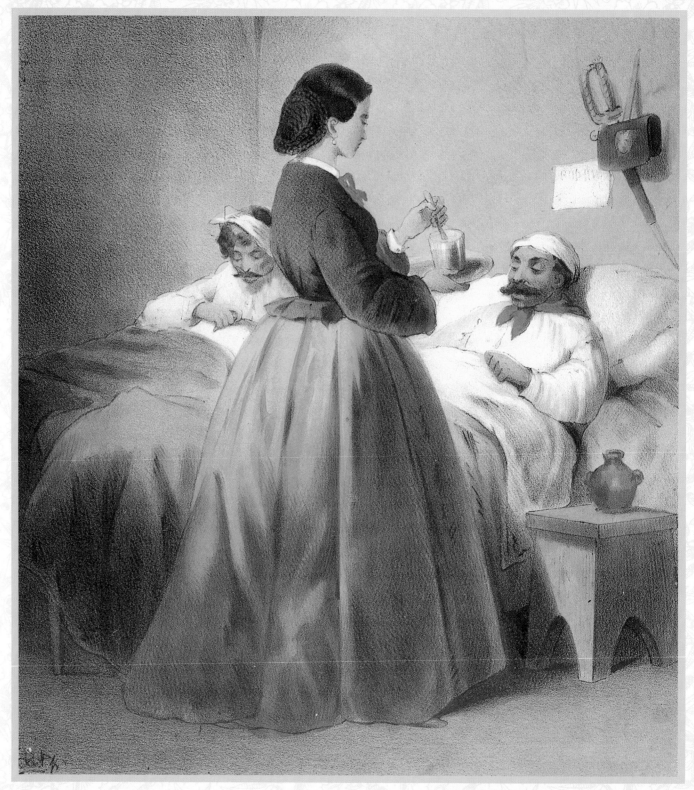

Florence Nightingale at Sartari, ANONYMOUS (C. 1854)

✢ 22 ✢

1967 *Birth of Eleanor McEvoy, Irish singer-songwriter*

✢ 23 ✢

1834 *Opening of St Vincent's Hospital, Dublin*

✢ 24 ✢

1862 *Birth of Edith Wharton, American novelist*

✢ 25 ✢

No one can make you feel inferior without your consent
ELEANOR ROOSEVELT

✢ 26 ✢

1928 *Birth of Eartha Kitt, American singer and actress*

✢ 27 ✢

1944 *Birth of Mairead Corrigan-Maguire, Irish co-founder of the Peace People*

✢ 28 ✢

I do not love thee! – no! I do not love thee!
And yet when thou are absent I am sad …
from *I Do Not Love Thee*, CAROLINE NORTON

There is no sea so deep, my
own, no mountain so high,
That I should not come to
you if I heard you cry.

There is no hell so sunken,
no heaven so steep,
Where I should not seek my
own, find you and keep.

from *Maternity*
KATHARINE TYNAN

> *M*uch enjoyment, and in some cases great benefit, might be obtained, at very little trouble or expense, if a few congenial friends arranged to meet once a week for reading, discussion, music, games, or any other amusement mutually agreed upon.
>
> from *Social Evenings*
> 19th century women's
> magazine article

❖ 29 ❖

1939 *Birth of Germaine Greer, Australian author and feminist*

❖ 30 ❖

1845 *Birth of Katharine Wood, better known as Kitty O'Shea,*
English mistress and later wife of Irish leader Charles Stewart Parnell

❖ 31 ❖

1864 *Birth of Matilda Knowles, internationally respected Irish botanist*
1885 *Birth of Anna Pavlova, Russian prima ballerina*

O had you seen the Coolun
Walking down by the cuckoo's street,
With the dew of the meadow shining
On her milk-white twinkling feet!
My love she is, and my colleen oge,
And she dwells in Bal'nagar;
And she bears the palm of beauty bright
From the fairest that in Erin are.

from *The Coolun*, trans. SAMUEL FERGUSON

Hugging the Old Illusion warm and dear,
The Silence and the Wise Book and the Lamp.
EVA GORE-BOOTH

La Belle Dame Sans Merci, WALTER CRANE (1845–1915)

An Irish Woman's

❦∥ℱEBRUARY ∥❦

We are the gentle people:
The passing dust we are,
With gusty laughter blowing
Near and far.
We are the gentle people,
Nor deal in praise or blame,
But we stand before your sorrow,
And we stand behind your shame.

NORA HOPPER CHESSON

FEBRUARY

❧ 1 ❧
1982 Ban on corporal punishment in Republic of Ireland schools came into effect

---
❧ 2 ❧
1650 Birth of Nell Gwyn, British actress and royal mistress

❧ 3 ❧
1896 Death of Lady Jane Wilde, Irish author who wrote under the pen name 'Speranza'

❧ 4 ❧
1865 Birth of Maud Gonne MacBride, Irish revolutionary and republican campaigner
1868 Birth of Constance Markievicz, Irish revolutionary

❧ 5 ❧
1829 Coombe Lying-in Hospital opens in Dublin
1921 Death of Katharine (Kitty) O'Shea, wife of Irish leader Charles Stewart Parnell

---
❧ 6 ❧
Rain in February is as good as manure
TRADITIONAL PROVERB

❧ 7 ❧
1924 Birth of Dora Bryan, British comedy actress

LEFT: *Fair Rosamund and Queen Eleanor*, SIR EDWARD COLEY BURNE-JONES (1833–1898)

Faraway Thoughts, CHARLES WEST COPE (1811–1890)

February

8

1926 *First performance of Sean O'Casey's* The Plough and the Stars *at the Abbey Theatre, Dublin, leads to rioting three nights later*

9

Triur gan riaghal – bean, múile agus muc
IRISH PROVERB

10

1818 *Death of Lady Eleanor Palmer, noted Irish beauty*

11

1984 *Closure of Royal Hibernian Hotel, Dublin*

12

1934 *Birth of Mary Quant, British fashion designer*

13

1827 *Birth of Sister Julia McGroarty, Irish founder of Trinity College, Washington D.C.*

14

1853 *The* Queen Victoria *sinks in a snowstorm off Howth Head. Fifty-five lives lost.*

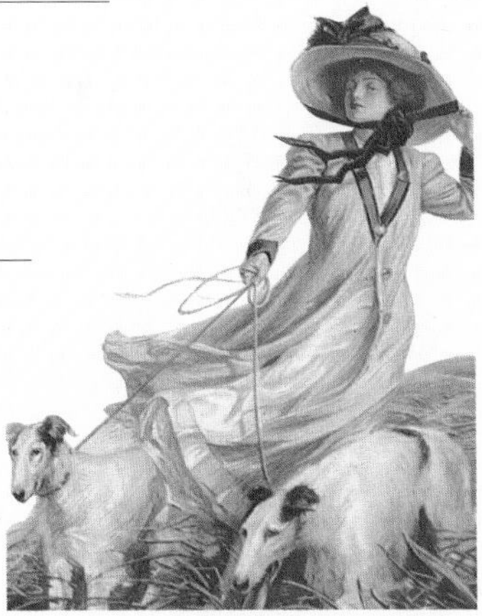

*Over the dim blue hills
Strays a wild river,
Over the dim blue hills
Rests my heart ever.
Dearer and brighter than
Jewels and pearl,
Dwells she in beauty
      there
Máire my girl.*

JOHN KEEGAN CASEY

Flower Arrangement (Teatime), SYDNEY MUSCHAMP (fl. 1884–1904)

15

1971 *Decimal day: Irish currency officially changed over to the decimal system*

16

She's descended from a long line her mother listened to.
GYPSY ROSE LEE

17

1944 *Birth of Brenda Fricker, Oscar-winning Irish actress*
1980 *The Derrynaflan Chalice and other ancient treasure discovered in Co. Tipperary*

18

1931 *Birth of Toni Morrison, American author*

19

1911 *Birth of Merle Oberon (Estelle Marie O'Brien Thompson), Tasmanian film actress*

20

I am righteously indignant, you are annoyed, she is making a fuss about nothing
ANON.

21

'Shut up!' Mother explained
ANON.

Some hours we should find for the pleasures of the mind
VICTORIAN PROVERB

FEBRUARY

❧ 22 ❧

1832 *First burial in Glasnevin Cemetery, Dublin*

❧ 23 ❧

1943 *Thirty-five orphan girls die in a fire at St Joseph's Orphanage, Cavan town*

❧ 24 ❧

1920 *Nancy Astor becomes the first woman to speak in the House of Commons*

❧ 25 ❧

1890 *Birth of Dame Myra Hess, British concert pianist*

❧ 26 ❧

One good turn gets most of the blanket
OLD SAYING

❧ 27 ❧

Fiadhnaise a' ghiolla bhréagaigh a bhean
IRISH PROVERB

❧ 28/29 ❧

1938 *Birth of Alice Taylor, Irish author (28th)*

*When I was young the days
were long,
Oh, long the days when I
was young:
So long from morn to evenfall
As they would never end
at all.*

from The Flying Wheel
KATHARINE TYNAN

But it is especially in the treatment of women by men that chivalry is always supposed to show itself. How may this be with us now? We fear it is a very enigmatical thing, this same masculine chivalry of the nineteenth century. In the humbler ranks it never induces men to prevent women from doing the hardest and coarsest labour. They may sweep crossings and fill coal trucks … and no chivalry says 'Leave it for me!'

FRANCES POWER COBBE

Fantasia in White, ALBERT LUDOVICI (1820–1894)

An Irish Woman's

MARCH

Some say he's dark,
I say he's bonny,
He's the flower of them all
My handsome, coaxing Johnny.

I know where I'm going,
I know who's going with me,
I know who I love,
But the dear knows who I'll marry.

TRADITIONAL SONG

1

1905 *Birth of Nano Reid, Irish artist*
1942 *Birth of Aine Hyland, Irish educationalist*

2

1950 *Birth of Karen Carpenter, American singer*

3

1854 *Death of Harriet Smithson, Irish actress who
captivated the composer Hector Berlioz*

4

It's the jewel that can't be got that is the most beautiful
TRADITIONAL PROVERB

5

*Would but indulgent Fortune send
To me a kind, and faithful friend*
MARY CHUDLEIGH

6

1944 *Birth of Dame Kiri Te Kanawa, New Zealand opera singer*

*Do good to your enemy, that
he may become your friend.
Do good to your friend, that
he remain your friend.*

ANON.

Nothing ever was half so tiresome as musical parties: no one gives them except those who can exhibit themselves, and fancy they excel ...: except that all the world of fashion are there, I would never go to another; for, positively, it is ten times more fatiguing than staying at home. To be compelled to look charmed, and to applaud, when you are half-dead from suppressing yawns, and to see half-a-dozen very tolerable men, with whom one could have a very pleasant chat, except for the stupid music, is really too bad.

from *Journal of a Lady of Fashion*
THE COUNTESS OF BLESSINGTON

LEFT: *Pink Blossom*, HAROLD H. PIFFARD (fl. 1895–1899)

7

1920 *Birth of Eilis Dillon, Irish novelist best known for* Across the Bitter Sea
1736 *Birth of Marie-Louise O'Morphi, Irish courtesan, mistress of King Louis XV of France*

8

1770 *Birth of Mary Ann McCracken, lover of Thomas Russell,
'The Man From God Knows Where'*

9

The more I see of men, the better I like dogs
MME ROLAND

10

Nobility listens to art
IRISH PROVERB

La Primavera,
detail of *Spring,* SANDRO
BOTTICELLI
(1445–1510)

*Summer Evening at Skagen, the Artist's Wife
with a Dog on a Beach*
PETER SEVERIN KROYER (1851-1909)

11

*1953 Birth of Mary Harney, Irish politician, the first woman
to lead a party in Dáil Éireann*

12

1946 Birth of Liza Minnelli, American actress and singer

13

General notions are generally wrong
LADY MARY WORTLEY MONTAGU

> *One half of the world
> cannot understand the
> pleasures of the other.*
>
> JANE AUSTEN

⊰ 14 ⊱

1985 *Two schoolchildren in Asdee, Co. Kerry, report*
that the local Marian statue had 'moved'

⊰ 15 ⊱

1852 *Birth of Lady Gregory, Irish playwright, author*
and co-founder of Dublin's Abbey Theatre

⊰ 16 ⊱

1896 *First use of X-rays in Ireland, at Dr Steevens's Hospital, Dublin*

The little waves of
Breffny go stumbling
through my soul.

EVA GORE-BOOTH

⊰ 17 ⊱

Saint Patrick's Day
1864 *Birth of Charlotte Milligan Fox, folk music collector and author*

⊰ 18 ⊱

1956 *Marriage of Prince Rainier of Monaco and*
Grace Kelly, Irish-American film actress

⊰ 19 ⊱

The beauty of a chaste woman makes bitter words
IRISH PROVERB

A Lady of Leisure, FREDERIC SOULACROIX (1825–1879)

---❖ 20 ❖---

1872 *Birth of Karin Michaelis, Danish author and feminist*

---❖ 21 ❖---

1970 *Dana brings Ireland victory in the Eurovision Song Contest for the first time*
1884 *Birth of Nora Barnacle, wife of the novelist James Joyce*

---❖ 22 ❖---

1848 *Birth of Sarah Purser, Irish artist*
1768 *Birth of Melasina Trench, Irish author*

---❖ 23 ❖---

1908 *Birth of Joan Crawford, American film actress and dancer*

---❖ 24 ❖---

1968 *Tuskar Rock air-disaster, Co. Wexford. Sixty-one killed.*

---❖ 25 ❖---

Ní'l nídh níos géire 'na teanga mná
IRISH PROVERB

---❖ 26 ❖---

1944 *Birth of Diana Ross, American actress and singer*

Hope is the thing with
feathers
That perches in the soul
And sings the tune
without the words
And never stops at all.

EMILY DICKINSON

❧ 27 ❧

1872 *Birth of Mary MacSwiney, Irish republican*

❧ 28 ❧

1686 *First pensioners admitted to the Royal Hospital, Kilmainham*
1824 *Death of Catherine Wilmot, Irish traveller and diarist*

❧ 29 ❧

1873 *Birth of Peig Sayers, renowned storyteller*
1793 *Death of Charlotte Brooke, author and Ulster folksong collector*

❧ 30 ❧

Want is the mistress of invention
Mrs Centlivre

❧ 31 ❧

*A misty winter brings a pleasant spring,
a pleasant winter, a misty spring.*
Traditional Rhyme

*Kathleen mavourneen, the
gray dawn is breaking
The horn of the hunter is
heard on the hill,
The lark from her light
wing the bright dew is
shaking —
Kathleen mavourneen,
what, slumbering still?
Oh hast thou forgotten
how soon we must sever?
Oh hast thou forgotten this
day we must part?
It may be for years, it
may be forever;
Oh why art thou silent,
thou voice of my heart?*

Louisa Crawford

An Irish Woman's

APRIL

Believe me, comedy goes through the world better than tragedy, and, take it all in all, does rather less mischief.

MARIA EDGEWORTH

APRIL

1

1911 *Launch of the* Titanic *from Harland & Wolff shipyard, Belfast*

2

1902 *The first production of Yeats'* Cathleen ni Houlihan, *starring Maud Gonne*
1861 *Death of Katharine Tynan, Irish writer and poet*

3

1900 *Oldest surviving moving film in Ireland shows*
Queen Victoria's last visit to Dublin

4

1917 *Birth of Sheila Conroy, Irish trade unionist*
1951 *Birth of Twink (Adele King), popular singer and actress*

Stella and Flavia every hour
Unnumbered hearts surprise;
In Stella's soul lies all her
power,
And Flavia's in her eyes.

MARY BARBER

5

1869 *Birth of Margaret Tennant, Irish social work pioneer*

6

May we have the grace of God and may we die in Ireland
IRISH BLESSING

7

1915 *Birth of Billie Holiday, American jazz and blues singer*

Among the innocent recreations of the fireside, there are few more commendable and practicable than those afforded by what are severally termed Enigmas and Charades etc. Of these there are such a variety, that they are suited to every capacity; and they present this additional attraction, that ingenuity may be exercised in the invention of them, as well as their solution. Many persons who have become noted for their literary compositions may date the origin of their success to the time when they attempted the composition of a trifling enigma or charade.

Evening Pastimes
Victorian magazine

LEFT: *Going Down Stream*, DAVID WOODLOCK (1842–1929)

Amaryllis, or The Shepherdess, WILLIAM HOLMAN HUNT (1827–1910)

APRIL

❧ 8 ❧

Gach nidh daor mian gach mnaoi

IRISH PROVERB

❧ 9 ❧

1984 *Death of Leslie de Barra, Irish revolutionary and Red Cross official*

❧ 10 ❧

1940 *Birth of Gloria Hunniford, Irish broadcaster*

❧ 11 ❧

Love against Time: and Love hath won the race

ROSA MULHOLLAND

❧ 12 ❧

1737 *Margaret ('Peg') Woffington, Irish actress, plays Ophelia, her first serious role, at Smock Alley Theatre, Dublin*

❧ 13 ❧

1742 *Premiere of Handel's* Messiah *in Dublin*
1953 *Death of Alice Milligan, Irish poet and cultural revivalist*

Yes'm, old friends is always best, 'less you can catch a new one that's fit to make an old one out of!

SARAH ORNE JEWETT

❧ 14 ❧

1859 *Death of Lady Sydney Owenson Morgan, Irish novelist and activist in the cause of Catholic Emancipation*

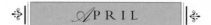

⁜ 15 ⁜

1882 *Birth of Mary Swanzy, Irish painter*
1912 *The luxury liner* Titanic *sinks off Newfoundland; of the 1500 who perish, 187 are Irish*

⁜ 16 ⁜

1939 *Birth of Dusty Springfield (Mary O'Brien), British singer*

⁜ 17 ⁜

1969 *Bernadette McAliskey (née Devlin) wins the Mid-Ulster by-election to become,*
at the age of 21, the youngest ever woman M.P.

⁜ 18 ⁜

1829 *Birth of Mother Mary Baptist Russell, Irish nun and first Superior of*
the Sisters of Mercy, California

Only choose in marriage a
man whom you would choose
as a friend were he a woman.

MARY FITZGERALD

⁜ SPERANZA'S LOVE ⁜

*I*n a few years such a collection would be impossible, for the old race is rapidly passing
away to other lands, and in the vast working world of America with all the new influences
of light and progress, the young generation, though still loving the land of their fathers, will
scarcely find leisure to dream over the fairy-haunted hills and lakes and raths of ancient
Ireland.

I must disclaim, however, all desire to be considered a melancholy Laudatrix
temporis acti. These studies of the Irish past are simply the expression of my love for the
beautiful island that gave me my first inspiration, my quickest intellectual impulses, and the
strongest and best sympathies with genius and country possible to a woman's nature.

LADY FRANCESCA SPERANZA WILDE in her Preface to *Ancient Legends of Ireland*

A Summer Reverie, HENRI MARTIN (1860–1943)

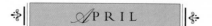

❖ 19 ❖

You can live without your own but not without your neighbour
IRISH PROVERB

❖ 20 ❖

Would you shackle spring to times and seasons?
AMY LOWELL

❖ 21 ❖

1816 *Birth of Charlotte Brontë, English novelist*

❖ 22 ❖

1894 *Birth of Evie Hone, Irish stained glass artist*

The Sleeping Beauty, THOMAS RALPH SPENCE (fl. 1876–1903)

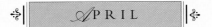

⚜ 23 ⚜

1947 *Birth of Bernadette McAliskey (née Devlin), Irish politician and civil rights activist*

⚜ 24 ⚜

1961 *Birth of Laura Magahy, Irish businesswoman, best known for spearheading the development of Dublin's Temple Bar area*

⚜ 25 ⚜

1892 *Birth of Mother Mary Martin, Irish founder of the Medical Missionaries of Mary*

Where we really love, we often dread more than we desire the solemn moment that exchanges hope for certainty.

MME DE STAËL

⚜ 26 ⚜

1979 *Grainne Cronin becomes the first woman pilot for Aer Lingus when she takes charge of the Frankfurt-Shannon flight*

Day-Dreams, JEAN BEAUDUIN (1851–1916)

❖ 27 ❖

1827 Birth of Mary Ward, Irish naturalist, artist and astronomer
1953 Death of Maud Gonne MacBride, Irish revolutionary beloved of Yeats

---

❖ 28 ❖

1875 Birth of Mother Kevin (Teresa Kearney), Irish missionary to Uganda
and founder of the Franciscan Missionary Sisters for Africa

❖ 29 ❖

Ah, 'All things come to those who wait.' They come, but often come too late.

LADY MARY M. CURRIE

❖ 30 ❖

Where is the man who has the power and skill
To stem the torrent of a woman's will?
For if she will, she will, you may depend on't;
And if she won't, she won't; so there's an end on't.

ANON.

So it is only by realising that unless the ideal, the spirit of self-sacrifice and love of country, is at the back of our work for commercial prosperity, sex emancipation, and other practical reforms, that we can hope to help our land. Every little act for Ireland's sake will help to build up a great nation, noble and self-sacrificing, industrious and free.

CONSTANCE MARKIEVICZ

I've had my soaring time,
my long, light day.

SUSAN MITCHELL

Lilies, WALTER CRANE (1845–1915)

An Irish Woman's

MAY

*I can see you young and glad
and wild,
May I never know you old
or changed.*

MARGARET MARY RYAN

MAY

⚜ 1 ⚜
1891 *Opening of Dublin Loop Line railway bridge*

⚜ 2 ⚜
1943 *Birth of Margaret (Maggie) Johnston, Irish champion bowls player*
1858 *Birth of Edith Somerville, Irish writer and artist*

⚜ 3 ⚜
1785 *First meeting of Irish Academy*
(Royal Irish Academy from 1786)

⚜ 4 ⚜
1773 *Art O'Leary killed by British soldiers near Macroom, Co. Cork,*
which moved his widow Eileen to compose her famous lament

⚜ 5 ⚜
1942 *Birth of Tammy Wynette, American country and western singer*

⚜ 6 ⚜
A woman like a lamb, a quiet, friendly woman
IRISH PROVERB

⚜ 7 ⚜
1915 *The luxury liner Lusitania is torpedoed by a German U-boat off Kinsale, Co. Cork,*
seven days after leaving New York. Over a thousand lose their lives.
1931 *Foundation of An Óige, the Irish Youth Hostel Association*

Joy often comes after sorrow, like morning after night

PEGGY O'BRIEN

Now and then you meet a person so exactly formed to please, that she will gain upon every one that hears or beholds her: this disposition is not merely the gift of nature, but frequently the effect of much knowledge of the world, and a command over the passions.

from *The Art of Being Agreeable* 1885

LEFT: *Young Friends*, LEXDEN LEWIS POCOCK (1850–1919)

MAY

8

1883 *Birth of Mary Elizabeth (Molly) Walker – Máire Nic Shiubhlaigh –
Irish republican and actress*

9

1936 *Birth of Glenda Jackson, British film actress*

10

1943 *Nineteen people killed when a 500-pound mine
exploded without warning at Ballymanus Bay, Co. Donegal*

11

An inch is a great deal on a nose
IRISH PROVERB

Reflections, WALTER PLIMPTON (fl. 1865–1890)

⁜ 12 ⁜

1712 *Building starts on Trinity College library, costing £15,000*
1944 *Death in Nairobi, Kenya, of Edel Mary Quinn, aged 36,*
Irish Legion of Mary envoy to East Africa

⁜ 13 ⁜

1982 *Tras Honan elected the first female Cathaoirleach of the Seanad*

They say there's bread
and work for all,
And the sun shines always
there:
But I'll not forget old
Ireland,
Were it fifty times as fair.

from *The Irish Emigrant*
LADY DUFFERIN

Possibly you have heard that I am, by divine indignation, a sort of author … and it is quite true. With Ireland in my heart, and epitomising something of her humour and her sufferings in my own character and story, I do trade upon the materials she furnishes me, and turning my patriotism into pounds, shillings and pence, endeavour at the same moment to serve her and support myself.

from *Florence Macarthy*
LADY SYDNEY MORGAN

⁜ 14 ⁜

Vanity, like murder, will out
HANNAH COWLEY

15

A woman can beat the devil

IRISH PROVERB

16

1920 *Start of three-day 'soviet' by workers at Knocklong creamery, Co. Limerick*
1955 *Birth of Olga Korbut, Russian Olympic gymnast*

17

1911 *Birth of Maureen O'Sullivan, Irish film actress*

18

1919 *Birth of Margot Fonteyn (Margaret Hookham), British prima ballerina*

19

1882 *Birth of Mary Hayden, Irish historian, campaigner for women's rights*

20

1790 *Death of Elizabeth Gunning, Duchess of Hamilton and Argyll, celebrated Irish beauty, so lovely that people once queued through the night to see her face*

21

1910 *Death of Mary Anne Kelly, Irish poet 'Eva' of* The Nation *newspaper*
1944 *Birth of Mary Robinson, first woman President of Ireland*

*I love, I love it; and who
shall dare
To chide me for loving that
old arm chair?*

from The Old Arm Chair
ELIZA COOK

*Oh Dear Heart, life
holds no gift
Half so precious, half
so brittle,
As this Love-cup that
we lift.*

ETHNA CARBERY

A Pensive Mood, ROGER-JOSEPH JOURDAIN (1845–1918)

MAY

22

1864 *Birth of Mother Mary Anne Cosgrave, Irish nun and Rhodesian pioneer*
1870 *Birth of Eva Gore Booth, Irish poet, trade unionist and feminist*
1941 *Birth of Caitlín Maude, Irish poet, actress, singer and political campaigner*

23

1903 *Birth of Shelah Richards, Irish actress and director*

24

1923 *Birth of Siobhán McKenna, Irish actress*
1955 *Birth of Maura 'Soshin' O'Halloran, Irish Buddhist nun and saint*

25

1842 *Birth of Helen Blackburn, Irish pioneer of feminism, trade unionist and author*

26

1920 *Birth of Peggy Lee (Norma Egstrom), American singer*

27

1943 *Birth of Cilla Black (Priscilla White), British singer*

A HERALD OF SPRING

MAY

❧ 28 ❧

1929 *Death of Alice Stopford Green, Irish historian and author*

❧ 29 ❧

1884 *Constance Mary Lloyd married Oscar Wilde*

❧ 30 ❧

1986 *Official opening for Connacht Regional Airport at Knock, Co. Mayo,*
now Horan International Airport

❧ 31 ❧

1889 *Birth of Helen Waddell, Irish medieval scholar, poet and author*
1937 *Birth of Mary O'Rourke, Irish politician*

> *Come when you're called;*
> *And do as you're bid;*
> *Shut the door after you*
> *And you'll never be chid.*
>
> MARIA EDGEWORTH

Feeding the Ducks, LOUIS ANTOINE AUGUSTE THOMAS (fl. c. 1865)

An Irish Woman's

JUNE

*Will you stand by the seas and
behold this place
As I shall stand when you're
far away?*

MARGARET MARY RYAN

❧ 1 ❧

1926 *Birth of Marilyn Monroe (Norma Jean Baker), American film actress*

❧ 2 ❧

1829 *Death, aged 90, of Lady Eleanor Butler, Irish recluse and one of the two celebrated 'Ladies of Llangollen'*

❧ 3 ❧

1878 *Birth of Sinéad Flanagan, wife of Éamon de Valera*

❧ 4 ❧

1864 *Birth of Ellen Lucy O'Brien (Neilí Ní Bhrian), Irish Gaelic Leaguer and ecumenist*

All through the days of childhood the garden is our fairy-ground of sweet enchantment and innocent wonder.

E.V. BOYLE

❧ 5 ❧

1899 *Death of Margaret Anne Cusack, the 'Nun of Kenmare', in religion Sister Mary Frances Clare, described as 'Ireland's first suffragette'*

❧ AN IRISH BALL ❧

*T*he grand ball was given last Thursday, to the great contentment of the best company of both sexes. The men were gallant, the ladies were courteous! … the musicians and singers were dressed like Arcadian shepherds and shepherdesses, and placed among the rocks. If tea, coffee or chocolate were wanting, you held your cup to a leaf of a tree, and it was filled; and whatever you wanted to eat or drink, was immediately found on a rock, or on a branch, or in the hollow of a tree. The waiters were all in whimsical dress, and every lady as she entered the room had a fine bouquet presented to her. The whole was extremely well conducted; no confusion; and the ladies say, never was there seen so enchanting a place; but a few dissenters had the assurance to say it was no better than a puppet-show.

MRS MARY DELANY
1752

LEFT: *Daydreams*, NORMAN PRESCOTT-DAVIES (1862–1915)

JUNE

⁕ 6 ⁕

1932 *Birth of Miriam Hederman O'Brien, Irish policy consultant, broadcaster,
and a director of Allied Irish Banks*

⁕ 7 ⁕

1899 *Birth of Elizabeth Bowen, Irish novelist and short story writer*
1900 *Birth of Patricia Lynch, Irish author*

⁕ 8 ⁕

1978 *Naomi James becomes the first woman to sail solo
around the world via Cape Horn*

⁕ 9 ⁕

It is no secret that is known to three
IRISH PROVERB

Little deeds of kindness,
Little words of love,
Help to make earth happy
Like the heaven above.
JULIA A. FLETCHER
CARNEY

⁕ 10 ⁕

1922 *Birth of Judy Garland (Frances Ethel Gumm), American film actress and singer*

⁕ 11 ⁕

1862 *Birth of Violet Florence Martin, Irish novelist who wrote under the pen name Martin Ross*
1912 *Birth of Mary Lavin, Irish short story writer and novelist*

⁕ 12 ⁕

1929 *Birth of Anne Frank, Jewish diarist*

*For women there are,
undoubtedly, great
difficulties in the path, but
so much the more to
overcome. First, no woman
should say 'I am but a
woman!' But a woman!
What more can you
ask to be?*

MARIA MITCHELL

Au Bord de la Mer, FRANÇOIS FLAMENG (1856–1923)

❖ 13 ❖

1699 *Funeral took place of 29-year-old Molly Malone, Dublin fishmonger renowned*
as the subject of the ballad 'Cockles and Mussels'
1884 *Birth of Mary Colum, Irish writer*

❖ 14 ❖

An áit m-biann caint, a's an áit a m-bhiann géidh biann callán

IRISH PROVERB

❖ 15 ❖

1920 *Birth of Amy Clampit, American poet*

'Tis the idle that grow
weary.
Gaily rings each
busy sound;
'Tis a pleasure to
be active;
There's a joy in labour
found.

MRS C. F. ALEXANDER

❖ 16 ❖

1904 *Nora Barnacle first walked out with James Joyce, and in tribute to her*
he set the action of his novel Ulysses *on this date*

❖ 17 ❖

1845 *Birth of Emily Lawless, Irish poet, historian and biographer*

❖ 18 ❖

1929 *Birth of Eva Bartok, Hungarian film actress*

❖ 19 ❖

1936 *Birth of Mary Holland, Irish political journalist, renowned for*
her coverage of Northern Ireland
1939 *Birth of Sister Stanislaus Kennedy, founder and president of Focus Point,*
campaigner for the homeless

JUNE

⅌ 20 ⅌

1906 *Birth of Catherine Cookson, British novelist*
1945 *Birth of Anne Murray, Canadian singer*

> *Be careful of the words*
> *you say, keep them soft*
> *and sweet; you never*
> *know from day to day*
> *which one's you'll*
> *have to eat ....*
>
> ANON.

⅌ 21 ⅌

1798 *Battle of Vinegar Hill, Enniscorthy, Co. Wexford,*
effectively the end of the 1798 Rising in Wexford

⅌ 22 ⅌

Never take a wife who has no fault
IRISH PROVERB

⅌ 23 ⅌

1802 *Mary O'Connell secretly marries her cousin Daniel O'Connell,*
later to be known as 'The Liberator'
1825 *Birth of Annie French Hector, Irish writer*

⅌ 24 ⅌

1874 *Birth of Úna Ní Fhaircheallaigh (Agnes O'Farrelly),*
Irish feminist, writer and Gaelic Leaguer

⅌ 25 ⅌

1891 *Katharine (Kitty) O'Shea married Charles Stewart Parnell*

How break away? If I was sure of myself and knew I could succeed for sure and make a name or more to the point money, I would bolt, live on a crust and do. But to do all that with the chance of having to return and throw oneself on the charity of one's family a miserable failure is more than I can screw up my courage to face. So many people begin with great promise…

CONSTANCE MARKIEVICZ

The Flower Maiden, HENRY JOHN STOCK (1853–1930)

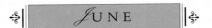

❖ 26 ❖

1892 *Birth of Pearl Buck, American author*

❖ 27 ❖

1922 *Birth of Marie Kean, Irish actress well known as Mrs Kennedy in the radio programme*
The Kennedys of Castle Ross

❖ 28 ❖

Your success and happiness lie in you
HELEN KELLER

❖ 29 ❖

1820 *The Dublin Society becomes the Royal Dublin Society*

❖ 30 ❖

Falaigheann gradh gráin, agus chi fúath a lán
IRISH PROVERB

After ecstasy, the laundry.
ZEN STATEMENT

*A well-kept house is a sign
of a misspent life.*
KITCHEN PLAQUE

*A woman cannot
guarantee her heart, even
though her husband be
the greatest and most
perfect of men.*

GEORGE SAND

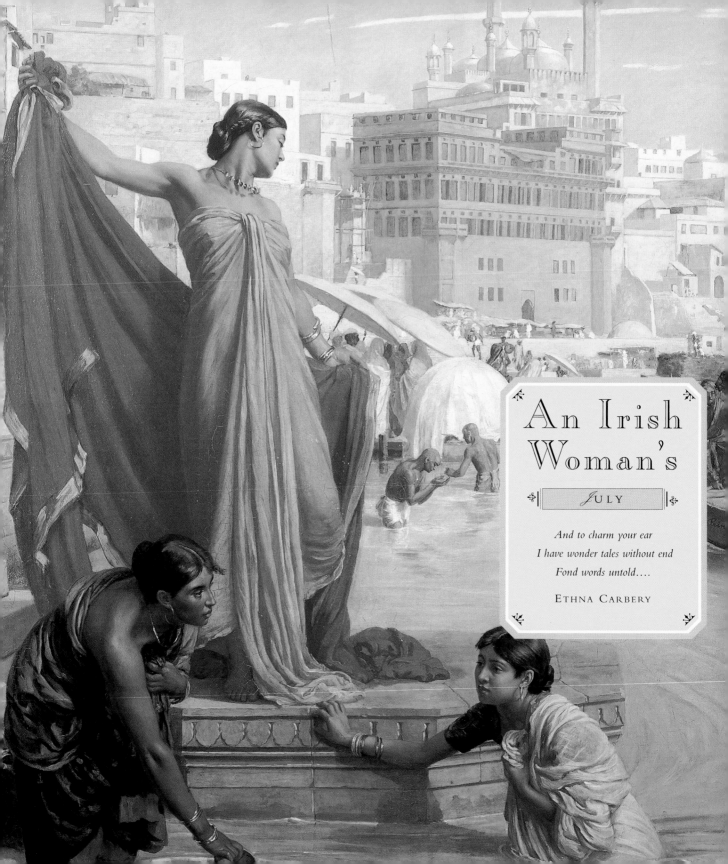

An Irish Woman's

JULY

And to charm your ear
I have wonder tales without end
Fond words untold....

ETHNA CARBERY

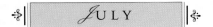

JULY

⸙ 1 ⸙

1804 *Birth of George Sand (Amandine Dupin), French novelist*
1961 *Birth of Princess Diana, former wife of the Prince of Wales*

⸙ 2 ⸙

1970 *Irish Catholic hierarchy announced it was no longer obligatory to*
abstain from eating meat on Fridays

⸙ 3 ⸙

Kiss me, kill me, love me, leave me, –
Damn me, dear, but don't deceive me!
EDITH NESBIT

⸙ 4 ⸙

Often was ugly amiable and pretty sulky
IRISH PROVERB

⸙ 5 ⸙

1958 *Birth of Veronica Guerin, Irish investigative reporter*

⸙ 6 ⸙

1939 *Birth of Mary Peters, Irish Olympic athlete*
1907 *Irish Crown jewels stolen and never recovered*

> *Love is like the wild-rose briar, friendship is like the holly-tree. The holly is dark when the rose briar blooms, but which will bloom most constantly?*
> EMILY BRONTË

> *A*llowing children to talk incessantly is a mistake. We do not mean to say that they should be restricted from talking in proper seasons, but they should be taught to know when it is proper for them to cease.
>
> from *Golden Hints for Housewives and Home Comforts*
> Magazine article c. 1913

LEFT: *Bathing in the Ganges*, VALENTINE CAMERON PRINSEP (1838–1904)

---------- ❧ 7 ❧ ----------

1739 *Death of Christian Davis, Irish female soldier, who enlisted to find her husband who had been press-ganged into the British army. She found him thirteen years later.*

---------- ❧ 8 ❧ ----------

1770 *Birth of Mary Ann McCracken, Irish patriot and philanthropist*

---------- ❧ 9 ❧ ----------

1959 *Mary Browne becomes the first Irish ban gharda (policewoman)*

---------- ❧ 10 ❧ ----------

1949 *Last-ever tram leaves from Nelson Pillar, Dublin*

> *Laziness may appear attractive, but work gives satisfaction.*
>
> MARY BARBER

> *The dead who died for*
> *Ireland*
> *Let not their memory die,*
> *But solemn and bright, like*
> *stars at night,*
> *Be they throned for aye*
> *on high.*
>
> ELLEN O'LEARY

Summer Evening on the Skagen Southern Beach
PETER SEVERIN KROYER (1851–1909)

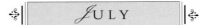

⟡ 11 ⟡

1817 *Act of Parliament establishes the first public lunatic asylums in Ireland*

⟡ 12 ⟡

1796 *First Orange Order 'Twelfth' demonstration was held*

⟡ 13 ⟡

1985 *Live Aid concert raises £45 million for Third World famine victims*

> *Mothers kept the peace in families. Everything goes back to the mother. It still does.*
>
> LILY FOY,
> born and bred in
> The Liberties, Dublin

⟡ 14 ⟡

Twenty years a-growing; twenty years at rest; twenty years declining; and twenty years when it doesn't matter whether you're there or not.

IRISH PROVERB

The Letter, JOHN TOWNSEND (BORN 1929)

*Youth's illusions, one by one
Have passed like clouds
That the sun looked on.*

D.F. MACARTHY

⸙ 15 ⸙

1919 *Birth of Iris Murdoch, Irish philosopher and novelist*
1927 *Death of Countess Markievicz, Irish revolutionary*

⸙ 16 ⸙

*And that my delight may be solidly fixed,
Let the friend and the lover be handsomely mixed*

LADY MARY WORTLEY MONTAGU

⸙ 17 ⸙

1884 *Birth of Louise Gavan Duffy, Irish educator and revolutionary*

⸙ 18 ⸙

1951 *Fire destroys the old Abbey Theatre in Dublin*

⸙ 19 ⸙

Solitude is the nurse of wisdom
OLD PROVERB

⸙ 20 ⸙

1882 *Death of Fanny Parnell, poet and co-founder of the Ladies' Land League.
Sister of Charles Stewart Parnell*

Mighty is the force of motherhood! It transforms all things by its vital heat; it turns timidity into fierce courage, and dreadless defiance into tremulous submission; it turns thoughtfulness into foresight, and yet stills all anxiety into calm content; it makes selfishness become self-denial, and gives even to hard vanity the glance of admiring love.

from *The Mill on the Floss*, GEORGE ELIOT

The Prelude, WILLIAM WARDLAW LAING (fl. 1873–1898)

21

May the Lord keep you in his hand and never close his fist too tight on you
IRISH BLESSING

22

1860 Birth of Mother Marie Joseph Butler, Irish educator, founder of the Marymount
schools and colleges in the USA and Europe

23

1803 Robert Emmet's uprising in Dublin begins and ends in a day

24

1898 Birth of Amelia Earhart, American pioneer aviator

25

The glowing ruby should adorn those who in warm July are born
ANON.

Just even to sit in a quiet church can take an awful lot off your mind.

UNA SHAW

26

1914 British troops open fire on a crowd at Bachelor's Walk, Dublin,
killing four and wounding 37

27

1669 Christening of Molly Malone, celebrated Irish fishmonger and subject of a ballad which
became Dublin's anthem, at St Werburgh's Church

The difference between rising every morning at six o'clock or eight, in the course of forty years, amount to 29,200 hours, or three years one hundred and twenty-one days and sixteen hours, which are equal to eight hours a day for exactly ten years. So that rising at six will be the same as if ten years of life (a weighty consideration) were added, wherein we may command eight hours every day for the cultivation of our minds and the despatch of business.

Early Rising from
ENQUIRE WITHIN UPON
EVERYTHING, 1902

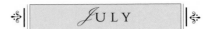

JULY

❖ 28 ❖

1943 *Cloghane air disaster, Co. Kerry, when ten died as a plane crashed*
onto the slopes of Mount Brandon

❖ 29 ❖

Give God the praise for any well spent day

❖ 30 ❖

Women are the real architects of society
Harriet Beecher Stowe

❖ 31 ❖

1834 *First train runs in Ireland from Dublin to Kingstown, drawn by horses*
1893 *Foundation of the Gaelic League to promote the Irish language*

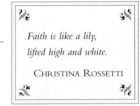

Faith is like a lily,
lifted high and white.

Christina Rossetti

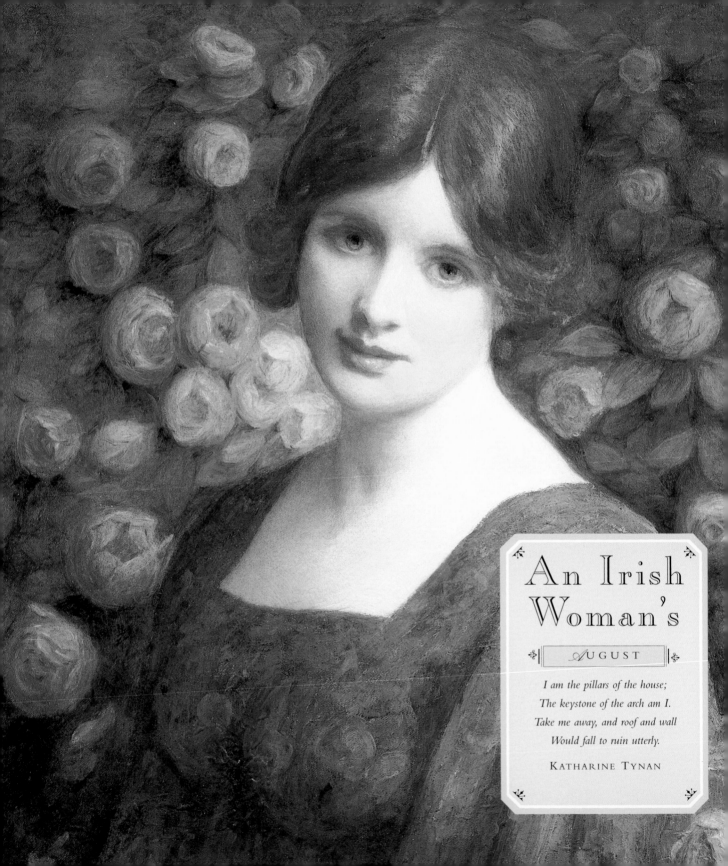

An Irish Woman's

AUGUST

I am the pillars of the house;
The keystone of the arch am I.
Take me away, and roof and wall
Would fall to ruin utterly.

KATHARINE TYNAN

AUGUST

⠶ 1 ⠶

1906 *Opening of Belfast City Hall*

⠶ 2 ⠶

1849 *Arrival in Ireland on a state visit of Queen Victoria, accompanied by Prince Albert and four children. She visited Belfast, Dublin and Cork.*

⠶ 3 ⠶

An ounce of mother-wit is worth a pound of clergy
SEVENTEENTH–CENTURY PROVERB

> *If we had no winter,
> the spring would not
> be so pleasant; if we
> did not sometimes taste
> of adversity, prosperity
> would not be so welcome.*
> ANNE BRADSTREET

⠶ 4 ⠶

1878 *Birth of Margaret Mary Pearse, Irish teacher, senator, sister of Patrick Pearse*

*A child is the
brightest ray in the
sunshine of a
parent's heart*

TRADITIONAL
SAYING

⠶ 5 ⠶

1823 *Royal Hibernian Academy of Arts receives its charter*

⠶ 6 ⠶

1830 *Opening of the first Dublin Horse Show*

⠶ 7 ⠶

1943 *Death of Sarah Purser, Irish artist, portrait painter and founder, in 1903, of the acclaimed studio for stained glass 'An Túr Gloine'*
1937 *Birth of Rosemary Smith, Irish international rally driver champion*

LEFT: *Innocent Youth*, TOM MOSTYN (1864–1930)

So many gods, so many
creeds
So many paths that wind
and wind,
While just the art of
being kind
Is all the sad world needs.
ELLA WILCOX

8

1879 *Birth of Eileen Gray, Irish architect and interior designer*
1953 *Opening of the Chester Beatty Library, Dublin*

9

1979 *First Vietnamese 'boat people' arrive in Ireland*

10

1976 *Peace Movement formed in Northern Ireland after the deaths
of three children in Belfast*

11

A child may have too much of her mother's blessing
OLD PROVERB

MY MOTHER BIDS ME BIND MY HAIR

My mother bids me bind my hair
With bands of rosy hue,
Tie up my sleeves with ribbons rare,
And lace my bodice blue.

'For why,' she cries, 'sit still and weep,
While others dance and play?'
Alas! I scarce can go or creep
While Lubin is away.

ANNE HUNTER

GRANT

The Sweet Smell of the Rose, ARTHUR GREENBANK (fl. 1880–1900)

Love's Spell, GEORGE FREDERICK CHESTER (fl. 1861–1889)

AUGUST

12
*1821 King George arrives in Ireland for a state visit
in an extremely drunken condition*

13
1974 Death of Kate O'Brien, Irish novelist and dramatist

*The dove will fly
From a ruined nest,
Love will not dwell
In a troubled breast;
The heart has no zest
To sweeten life's
        dolour
If Love, the Consoler,
Be not its guest!*

IRISH BALLAD

14
One look before is better than three looks behind
IRISH PROVERB

15
*1880 Derrybeg, Co. Donegal, flooding tragedy at a chapel where
five members of a congregation celebrating mass were drowned*

16
*1711 Opening of the medical school, laboratory and anatomical
theatre at Trinity College Dublin*

*What do I want of thee?
No gift of smile or tear
Nor casual company,
But in still speech to me
Only thy heart to hear.*

SUSAN MITCHELL

17
*1734 Ten-bed hospital opened by Mary Mercer in Dublin
1921 Birth of Maureen O'Hara (Maureen Fitzsimmons), Irish film actress*

18
*Backward, turn backward, O Time in thy flight;
Make me a child again, just for tonight*
ELIZABETH AKERS ALLEN

✠ AUGUST ✠

✠ 19 ✠

1883 *Birth of Coco Chanel (Gabriella Chanel), French fashion designer*

✠ 20 ✠

If you want to know me, come and live with me
IRISH PROVERB

> *We never know how high we are*
> *Till we are called to rise;*
> *And then, if we are true to plan,*
> *Our statures touch the skies.*
>
> EMILY DICKINSON

✠ 21 ✠

1854 *Last ever Donnybrook Fair*
1879 *Apparitions at Knock, Co. Mayo of the Virgin Mary seen by at least 22 people over two hours*

✠ 22 ✠

1893 *Birth of Dorothy Parker, American author and wit*

✠ 23 ✠

Do you remember yet, a gradh, the sunshine of that day…?
ETHNA CARBERY

✠ 24 ✠

*H*e used to say, 'Mother, if I ever win anything on the horses I'll bring you a gramophone'. Well, here one day me mother … sees the door opening and a big horn, and him carrying the thing. He was after winning £3.10. And bought the gramophone, His Master's Voice. Big, big green thing. Oh, we were charmed…. Me mother, she had brown eyes and they nearly fell out of her head. And she kept kissing him. The whole £3.10! On her. That's all he wanted. He idolised her.

MARY DOOLAN, former Dublin tenement resident

The Kiosk, FRANCIS JOHN WYBURD (fl. 1846–1893)

❖ 25 ❖

Read not books alone, but men; and above all, read thyself
VICTORIAN SAYING

❖ 26 ❖

1913 *First day of the Great 'Lock-Out' in Dublin. By the end of September, 100,000 Dubliners faced starvation.*

❖ 27 ❖

1910 *Birth of Mother Theresa of Calcutta, Yugoslavian nun*

At Clitheroe through the
sunset hour
My soul was very far away:
I saw Ben Bulben's rose
and fire
Shining afar o'er Sligo Bay.

EVA GORE-BOOTH

❖ 28 ❖

1815 *Birth of Mary Martin, Irish novelist*
1929 *Birth of Jackie Onassis, widow of President Kennedy*

❖ 29 ❖

1750 *Death of Laetitia Pilkington, Irish writer and adventurer*
1890 *Opening of the National Library of Ireland*

❖ 30 ❖

1841 *First published edition of* The Cork Examiner
1951 *Birth of Dana (Rosemary Brown), Irish singer*

❖ 31 ❖

Wear a sardonyx or for thee
No conjugal felicity.
The August-born without this stone
'Tis said must live unloved and lone.

ANON.

*A*n excellent medicine is brimstone and treacle, prepared by mixing an ounce and a half of sulphur, and half-an-ounce of cream of tartar, with eight ounces of treacle; and, according to the age of the child, giving from a small teaspoonful to a dessertspoonful early in the morning, two or three times a week....

'Summer Aperients for Children' from
ENQUIRE WITHIN UPON EVERYTHING, 1911

Comparing Cards, Anonymous (19/20th century)

An Irish Woman's

❦ SEPTEMBER ❧

*Rise from your knees, O
daughters, rise!
Our mother still is young and fair,
Let the world look into your eyes
And see her beauty shining there.*

from *To the Daughters of Erin*
SUSAN MITCHELL

SEPTEMBER

⚜ 1 ⚜

1737 *First edition of* The Belfast Newsletter, *Ireland's oldest daily newspaper*
1789 *Birth of Marguerite, Countess of Blessington, Irish novelist, beauty and gossip writer*
1830 *The Zoological Gardens, Dublin, the third oldest in the world, opened to the public*

⚜ 2 ⚜

To meet, worth parting for:

Bitter forgot in sweet.

CHRISTINA ROSSETTI

⚜ 3 ⚜

1850 *Establishment of Queen's Colleges in Belfast, Cork and Galway, now*
Queen's University, University College Cork and University College Galway

---

⚜ 4 ⚜

1935 *Birth of Pauline Bewick, Irish artist*
1989 *Century Radio, Ireland's first national commercial station, goes on the air*

⚜ 5 ⚜

1911 *Formation of the Irish Women Workers' Union*
1958 *Birth of Kathy Prendergast, Irish artist*

⚜ 6 ⚜

1911 *Birth of Lady Angela Christina McDonnell Antrim,*
Irish sculptor and cartoonist

⚜ 7 ⚜

1984 *Restoration of the Royal Hospital, Kilmainham, completed*

> *No entertainment is so cheap as reading, nor any pleasure so lasting.*
>
> LADY MARY
> WORTLEY MONTAGU

> *Of all the systems which human nature in its moments of intoxication has produced – if indeed a bundle of contradictions and absurdities may be called a system – that which men have contrived with a view to forming the minds, and regulating the conduct of women, is perhaps the most completely absurd.*
>
> MARY HAYS
> 1798

> How much more miserable
> we should be than we are
> if we had our eyes opened
> to discern always true from
> make-believe.
>
> GERALDINE JEWSBURY

8

1908 *St Enda's School opens under the headmastership of Patrick Pearse*

9

1649 *Siege of Drogheda, by Oliver Cromwell's army, begins*

10

1813 *Fall of Ireland's largest meteorite, the 'Limerick Stone' of 65 pounds*

11

There is no cure for love but marriage
IRISH PROVERB

Letter, with Quill Pen, ADOLPHE PIOT (c. 1890)

Finished 'Work', – twenty
chapters. Not what it should
be – too many interruptions.
Should like to do one book
in peace, and see if it
wouldn't be good.

LOUISA MAY ALCOTT
1872

The Annunciation, EDWARD REGINALD FRAMPTON (1872–1923)

♦ 12 ♦

It is one of the privileges of friendship to talk of our own follies and infirmities
LADY MARY WORTLEY MONTAGU

♦ 13 ♦

1845 Gardener's Chronicle and Horticultural Gazette *stops the presses to report the failure of the potato crop*

♦ 14 ♦

1866 *Birth of Alice Milligan, Irish writer, nationalist and Irish revivalist*
1907 *Birth of Edel Quinn, Irish Legion of Mary envoy to East Africa*

✣ 15 ✣

1976 *Mrs Anne Dickson becomes the first woman to lead an Irish political party,*
the Unionist Party of Northern Ireland
1974 *Death of Mrs Sydney Czira, née Sydney Gifford, Republican journalist*

✣ 16 ✣

Bionn an grádh caoch
IRISH PROVERB

✣ 17 ✣

1934 *Birth of Maureen Connolly (Little Mo), Irish-American tennis champion*

---

*P*rison. It was not
prison for me.
Hungerstrikes. They had
no fears for me. Cat and
Mouse Act. I could have
laughed. A prison cell was
quiet – no telephone, no
paper, no speeches, no sea
sickness, no sleepless nights.
I could lie on my plank bed
all day and all night and
return once more to my
daydreams.

ANNIE KENNEY
Suffragette

✣ 18 ✣

1851 *Death of Anne Devlin, Irish patriot and heroine, a committed rebel referred to as 'Robert*
Emmet's housekeeper' by historians

✣ 19 ✣

1757 *Opening of St Patrick's Hospital, Dublin, an asylum for the mentally ill*

✣ 20 ✣

1588 *Three ships of the Spanish Armada run aground at Streedagh, Co. Sligo*
1896 *Birth of Norah Hoult, Irish writer*

At twenty my complexion
was like alabaster, and at
five paces distant the
sharpest eyes could not
discover my pearl necklace
from my skin.

LADY HESTER
STANHOPE

✣ 21 ✣

Thou straggler into loving arms,
Young climber-up of knees,
When I forget thy thousand ways
Then life and all shall cease.

MARY LAMB

La Primavera, detail of the Three Graces, SANDRO BOTTICELLI (1445–1510)

SEPTEMBER

> *Sorry am I to say I have often observed that I have performed worst when I most ardently wished to do better than ever.*
>
> SARAH SIDDONS

✣ 22 ✣

1884 HMS Wasp *was wrecked off Tory Island with the loss of 52 lives*

✣ 23 ✣

To the whole world my tenderness be known
What is the world to her, who lives for thee alone.
MARTHA SANSOM

✣ 24 ✣

1861 *Opening of Mater Hospital, Dublin*
1944 *Birth of Eavan Boland, Irish poet*

✣ 25 ✣

Better good manners than good looks
IRISH PROVERB

✣ 26 ✣

1766 *Death of Frances Sheridan (née Chamberlaine), novelist, playwright and mother of Richard Brinsley Sheridan*
1873 *Birth of Anna Smithson, Irish novelist and nurse*

✣ 27 ✣

1972 *Opening of the National Institute for Higher Education, Limerick, now the University of Limerick*

The clouds had made a crimson
crown
Above the mountains high.
The stormy sun was going
down
In a stormy sky.

Why did you let your eyes so
rest on me
And hold your breath between?
In all the ages this can never be
As if it had not been.

A Moment
MARY ELIZABETH
COLERIDGE

❖ 28 ❖

1912 Ulster's Solemn League and Covenant was signed in Belfast by 237,368 men against Home Rule; 234,046 women signed a parallel declaration

---
❖ 29 ❖

1778 Birth of Catherine McAuley, Irish founder of the Order of Mercy
1908 Birth of Greer Garson, Academy-Award-winning Irish film actress

---
❖ 30 ❖

1959 World premiere of Mise Eire *at Cork Film Festival*

> *My dreams were all my own; I accounted for them to nobody; they were my refuge when annoyed, my dearest pleasure when free.*
> MARY SHELLEY

*B*ut no matter how poor they'd be on a Saturday night they'd be sitting outside. People'd all come around and sit on the steps and they'd get pig's legs or a pig's cheek or ribs and they shared it. Shared everything with one another. Same with births, deaths, and marriage, they all came. Everybody helped. Children would be out playing and the parents would be together. And we used to have a lot of street singers. There was a woman used to play the banjo and she'd come along and sing and there was a girl that'd play the violin and she was great …
just to sit and listen to her.

ELIZABETH 'BLUEBELL' MURPHY
former resident of a tenement on Corporation Street, Dublin

Elaine from la Mort d'Arthur, CHARLES EDWIN FRIPP (1854–1906)

An Irish Woman's

OCTOBER

'Twas the dream of a God
And the mould of his hand,
That you shook 'neath His stroke,
That you trembled and broke
To this beautiful land.

Ireland
DORA SIGERSON
SHORTER

OCTOBER

The wife who will establish the rule of allowing her husband to have the last word will achieve for herself and her sex a great moral victory! Is he right? – it were a great error to oppose him. Is he wrong? – he will soon discover it, and applaud the self-command which bore unvexed his pertinacity. And gradually there will spring up such a happy fusion of feelings and ideas, that there will be no 'last word' to contend about, but a steady and unruffled flow of generous sentiment.

from *'Counsels for Wives'*
Edwardian magazine
article, 1906

1

1911 *Unveiling of the Parnell Monument in O'Connell Street, Dublin*

2

1942 *The cruiser* Curaçao *sinks off the Co. Donegal coast with the loss of 338 lives after colliding with the liner* Queen Mary

3

1980 *Miss Justice Mella Carroll becomes the first female judge of the Irish High Court*

4

Mairg ná deineann cómhairle deaghmhná
IRISH PROVERB

5

1968 *Northern Ireland Civil Rights Association march in Derry*

6

1928 *Birth of Maeve Kyle, international athlete and hockey player*

To live happily, try to promote the happiness of others.

Advice to Young Ladies
Magazine article, c. 1911

7

Greatly shining,
The Autumn moon floats in the thin sky …
AMY LOWELL

LEFT: *The Tryst*, WILLIAM HOLYOAKE (1834–1894)

OCTOBER

8

1858 *Birth of Edith Somerville, Irish novelist*

9

1891 *Birth of Lil Nic Dhonnachachadha (Lilian Duncan)*
teacher and Irish language worker

10

1977 *Mairead Corrigan and Betty Williams, founders of the Peace Movement in Northern*
Ireland, win the Nobel Prize for Peace

11

1866 *Opening of Alexandra College for girls, Dublin*
1973 *Mary Tinney, Ireland's first woman ambassador, appointed to Sweden and Finland*

12

1969 *Death of Louise Gavan Duffy, pioneering educationalist; one of the first women to enter*
UCD and founder of Scoil Bhríde, the first all-Irish school for girls, Dublin, 1917

13

1981 *Publication of the first Irish-language version of the Bible for over 200 years*

14

1917 *Magdalen Hone, widow of Nathaniel Hone the artist, presents 500 of his oil paintings*
and 900 watercolours to the National Gallery of Ireland

Shall mine eyes behold thy
glory, O my country?
FANNY PARNELL

Carrying the Peacock, JOHN DAWSON WATSON (1832–1892)

OCTOBER

❖ 15 ❖
1889 Birth of Margaret Burke Sheridan ('Divine Diva'), Irish soprano

---
❖ 16 ❖
A foster child is as he is brought up
IRISH PROVERB

❖ 17 ❖
1907 Marconi telegraphy service starts between Clifden, Co. Galway, and Cape Breton, Canada

---
❖ 18 ❖
c. 1780 Birth of Peg Woffington, Irish actress

❖ 19 ❖
1913 Death of Emily Lawless, Irish novelist and poet

❖ 20 ❖
Up, maiden fair! and bind thy hair,
And rouse thee in the breezy air.
JOANNA BAILLIE

$\mathcal{O}$CTOBER

21
1917 *George Hyde-Lees, aged 26, marries the poet W. B. Yeats, aged 52*
1951 *First Wexford Opera Festival takes place*

22
1884 *First women graduates conferred by the Royal University of Ireland*

23
Whoso loves believes the impossible
ELIZABETH BARRETT BROWNING

24
1880 *First meeting of the Irish Ladies' Land League, founded by Fanny Parnell,
Jane Byrne and Ellen Ford in New York*

25
1968 *New University of Coleraine, Ulster, officially opens*

26
*Love me still but know not why, so hast thou the same reason still
to dote upon me ever.*
ANON.

27
1932 *Birth of Sylvia Plath, American poet and novelist*

The family was very powerful, you know, very comforting. And the extended family with the grannies. The granny was the matriarch. She minded the children and told everybody what to do. She was very powerful and much loved. The fathers never worked. Never worked. Whatever income was coming in was gained by the mothers …

PEGGY PIGOTT,
Northside Dublin
teacher in the 1950s

*Come the wind may
never again
Blow as it blows now
for us …*

EMILY BRONTË

When Sorrow Comes in Summer Days, Roses Bloom in Vain
JOHN MELHUISH STRUDWICK (1849–1937)

OCTOBER

--- ❖ 28 ❖ ---

1927 *Cleggan Disaster, when 16 fishermen drown off the coast of Galway, nine from Inishbofin*

--- ❖ 29 ❖ ---

1825 *Birth of Catherine Hayes, Irish opera singer known as the 'Irish Nightingale'*

--- ❖ 30 ❖ ---

1865 *Birth of Rose Mabel Young, Irish Gaelic scholar*

--- ❖ 31 ❖ ---

1883 *Birth of Sarah Allgood, Irish actress*

An Irish Woman's

NOVEMBER

No art I used men's love to draw;
I lived but by my being's law,
As roses are by heaven designed
To bring the honey to the wind.

KATHERINE BRADLEY
& EDITH COOPER

$\mathcal{N}$OVEMBER

❖ 1 ❖

Tástáil do dhuine muinteartha sul a dteastóidh sé uait
IRISH PROVERB

❖ 2 ❖

1952 Death of Molly Allgood, Irish actress

❖ 3 ❖

1969 Breathalyser introduced into the Republic

❖ 4 ❖

1974 Powerscourt House, Enniskerry, Co. Wicklow, destroyed by fire

---

❖ 5 ❖

1850 Birth of Ella Wheeler Wilcox, American feminist activist

---

❖ 6 ❖

Mankind should hope, in wedlock's state,
A friend to find as well as mate …
MARY SAVAGE

❖ 7 ❖

1878 Birth of Margaret Cousins (née Gillespie), Irish teacher and worker
for women's rights in India
1968 Senator Margaret Pearse accorded a state funeral

LEFT: *An Afternoon Ride in Hyde Park, London*, A.F. DE PRADES (fl. 1862–1879)

ℕOVEMBER

⇥ **8** ⇤

1900 *Birth of Margaret Mitchell, American writer*

⇥ **9** ⇤

1935 *Arranmore, Co. Donegal, boating tragedy, when 19 drown off Arranmore Island, 12 of these being islanders returning from a potato harvest in Scotland*

⇥ **10** ⇤

1896 *Birth of Lady Mary Heath, record-breaking Irish pioneer aviator and athlete*

⇥ **11** ⇤

1908 *Irish Women's Franchise League founded by Hanna Sheehy-Skeffington and Margaret Cousins*

⇥ **12** ⇤

1929 *Birth of Grace Kelly, Irish-American film actress and later Princess of Monaco*
1967 *First Rosc Art Exhibition at the Royal Dublin Society's H.Q., Ballsbridge, Dublin*

⇥ SWEET WICKLOW MOUNTAINS ⇤

Sweet Wicklow mountains! the sunlight sleeping
On your green banks is a picture rare,
You crowd around me, like young girls peeping,
And puzzling me to say which is most fair;
As tho' you'd see your own sweet faces,
Reflected in that smooth and silver sea,
Oh! my blessin' on those lovely places,
Tho' no one cares how dear they are to me.

from *Oh! Bay of Dublin*
LADY DUFFERIN

❧ NOVEMBER ❧

❧ **13** ❧

1831 *Sisters of Mercy established by Catherine McAuley*
1863 *St Stephen's Green open to the public*

LAMBERT & BUTLER'S CIGARETTES.
LADIES SKI-ING.

❧ **14** ❧

*Beauty is the possession of him to whom it is born, but it is manner
that captivates every one*

IRISH PROVERB

❧ **15** ❧

1887 *Birth of Georgia O'Keefe, American artist*

*H*umanity is like a
bird with its two
wings – the one is male,
the other female. Unless
both wings are strong and
impelled by some common
force, the bird cannot fly
heavenwards. According to
the spirit of this age,
women must advance and
fulfil their mission in all
departments of life,
becoming equal to men.
They must be on the same
level as men and enjoy
equal rights.

'ABDU'L BAHÁ

❧ **16** ❧

1986 *Death of Siobhán McKenna, Irish actress*

---

*Dread remorse when you
are tempted to err, Miss
Eyre: remorse is the
poison of life.*

CHARLOTTE BRONTË

❧ **17** ❧

1930 *First Irish Hospital Sweepstakes draw sees first prize of $208,792
shared between three winners*

❧ **18** ❧

1967 *Sculpture of Wolfe Tone unveiled at St Stephen's Green, Dublin*

❧ **19** ❧

1871 *Birth of Margaret Dobbs, Irish historian and Gaelic Leaguer*
1900 *Birth of Pamela Hinkson, Irish writer and daughter of Katharine Tynan*

20

1969 *Death of Josephine MacNeill, first Irish woman diplomatic representative abroad*

21

Tógh do chuideachta sul a suidhfir
IRISH PROVERB

22

1919 *Birth of Máire Drumm, Irish republican*

23

1819 *Birth of Margaret Aylward, Irish founder of the Sisters of the Holy Faith*
1845 *Birth of Charlotte O'Brien, Irish social reformer, botanist and writer*

She had a womanly instinct that clothes possess an influence more powerful over many than the worth of character or the magic of manners.

LOUISA MAY ALCOTT

NOVEMBER

❖ 24 ❖
Success is counted sweetest
By those who ne'er succeed

EMILY DICKINSON

Beyond, beyond the
mountain line,
The greystone and the
boulder,
Beyond the growth of dark
green pine,
That crowns its western
shoulder,
There lies that fairy land of
mine,
Unseen of a beholder.

from *Dreams*
MRS ALEXANDER

❖ 25 ❖
1906 *Birth of Saidie Paterson, Irish trade unionist and peace activist*

❖ 26 ❖
1794 *First Irish transported convicts arrive in New South Wales, Australia*

Give me a generous soul
that glows
With other's transports,
other's woes …

ELIZABETH RYVES

❖ 27 ❖
1871 *Gaiety Theatre, Dublin, opens with a production of* She Stoops to Conquer

❧ 28 ❧

Nothing is preferable to reconciliation

IRISH PROVERB

❧ 29 ❧

1832 *Birth of Louisa May Alcott, American author*

My love in her attire doth
show her wit,
It doth so well become her.

ANON.

❧ 30 ❧

1969 *Birth of Catherina McKiernan, champion Irish cross-country athlete*

Dressing from twelve to three. Madame Tornure sent me a most unbecoming cap: mem. I shall leave her off when I have paid her bill. Heigh-ho! when will that be? Tormented by duns, jewellers, mercers, milliners: I think they always fix on Mondays for dunning: I suppose it is because they know one is sure to be horribly vapored after a Sunday-evening's party, and they like to increase one's miseries.

from *Journal of a Lady of Fashion*
MARGUERITE, COUNTESS OF BLESSINGTON

Romantic Thoughts, WALTER ANDERSON (fl. 1856–1886)

An Irish Woman's

I cannot sing the old songs
I sang long years ago,
For heart and voice would fail me
And foolish tears would flow.

CHARLOTTE BARNARD

DECEMBER

❧ 1 ❧

1722 *Death of Susanna Centlivre, Irish playwright*

❧ 2 ❧

1811 *Kildare Place Society founded to organise non-denominational schools in Ireland*

❧ 3 ❧

1897 *Birth of Kate O'Brien, Irish author and playwright*
1990 *Mary Robinson installed as seventh President of Ireland*

❧ 4 ❧

1822 *Birth of Frances Power Cobbe, Irish essayist*
1887 *Birth of Winifred Carney, Irish socialist, trade unionist and revolutionary*

❧ 5 ❧

1830 *Birth of Christina Rossetti, English poet*

❧ ELLEN O'LEARY ❧
---

*S*he had grown old waiting for this little time of union with the brother who fulfilled her sternest ideals. Once she told me she had never been in love because she had never met a man like her brother. One could believe it, for there was something virginal about her, as if she had never known the little softness and folly of love … Yet with true love she had keen sympathy. One would not bare to her for worlds one's little follies and fancies, the vagrant preferences, the indiscretions, that most girls and women know of themselves and others. Love, with her, to be believed in, must have had more than an element of loftiness…. I have never known a woman so strong.

KATHARINE TYNAN

writing about her memory of Ellen O'Leary in *'An Exile's Sister'*

LEFT: *A Favourite Piece*, RAIMONDO DE MADRAZO (1841–1920)

ᴅ ᴇᴄᴇᴍʙᴇʀ

⟡ 6 ⟡
1920 Birth of Elizabeth (Lizzie) Crotty, Irish traditional musician
1922 Irish Free State comes into existence

⟡ 7 ⟡
Short and sweet like an ass's trot
Tʀᴀᴅɪᴛɪᴏɴᴀʟ Pʀᴏᴠᴇʀʙ

⟡ 8 ⟡
1542 Birth of Mary Queen of Scots

⟡ 9 ⟡
1969 The National Gallery of Ireland purchases Goya's 'The Dream' for £145,000

⟡ 10 ⟡
1830 Birth of Emily Dickinson, American poet

Not in vain is Ireland
pouring itself all over the
earth ... The Irish, with
their glowing hearts and
reverent credulity, are
needed in this cold age of
intellect and scepticism.

Lʏᴅɪᴀ Cʜɪʟᴅ

⟡ 11 ⟡
Oh my son's my son till he gets him a wife,
But my daughter's my daughter all her life.
Dɪɴᴀʜ Cʀᴀɪᴋ

⟡ 12 ⟡
1873 Birth of Lola Ridge, Irish poet and radical
1928 Issue of the new Free State currency

*She was then but
fourteen but her size
forced her to dress quite
Womanly—She led us into
a new Species of Culinary
Preparations—Namely
making up washes and
beautifying lotions—We had
two or three of the Tenants
every day hunting the
Country for different sorts
of Herbs, and such Plaisters
and Milk Washes as We
made up would be enough
to ruin all the fair Skins in
the Circassioan Marts—
Every night we were wrapd
up like Pomatum Sticks in
greasy brown Paper, and
I'm sure if any Stranger
had seen us at Night they
would have taken [us] for
three Egyptian Mummies
ready Embalmd.*

from *Retrospections
of an Outcast*
Dᴏʀᴏᴛʜᴇᴀ Hᴇʀʙᴇʀᴛ

In the Park, GEORGE DUNLOP LESLIE (1835–1921)

DECEMBER

❧ 13 ❧

1945 *Family Allowances Act (NI) provides for payment of 5s per week for second and subsequent children*
1952 *Adoption Act (RI) stipulates that adopters must be of the same religion as the adopted child*

❧ 14 ❧

1874 *Death of Biddy Early, Irish white witch*

❧ 15 ❧

1930 *Birth of Edna O'Brien, Irish novelist*

❧ 16 ❧

1911 *Local Authorities (Ireland) (Qualification of Women) Act allows women to become members of county and borough councils*

❧ 17 ❧

1834 *First railway in Ireland and the world's first suburban railway from Dublin to Kingstown (Dun Laoghaire) was opened*

❧ 18 ❧

Cha robh se air faghail, 'n úair a bhi an chiall da roinn
IRISH PROVERB

❧ 19 ❧

1973 *Irish Supreme Court rules against the prohibition of the importation of contraceptives*

There is nothing so strong as the force of love; there is no love so forcible as the love of an affectionate mother to her natural child.

ELIZABETH
GRYMESTON

One might say I had had already a sufficiently large share of the earth's beauties to enjoy, yet here opened out an utterly new and unique experience – Ireland. Our wedding tour was chiefly devoted to the Wild West, with a pause at Glencar, in Kerry. I have tried … to convey to my readers … my impression of that Western country – its freshness, its wild beauty, its entrancing poetry, and that sadness which, like the minor key in music, is the most appealing quality in poetry. … My husband had given me the choice of a locale for the wedding tour between Ireland and the Crimea. How could I hesitate?

from *A Soldier's Wife, an Autobiography*
LADY ELIZABETH BUTLER

❧ 20 ❧

1909 *Ireland's first cinema, The Volta, opens in Mary St, Dublin*

❧ 21 ❧

1915 *Death of Violet Martin, Irish novelist under the pen-name of Martin Ross*
1985 *Foundation of the Progressive Democratic Party*

❧ 22 ❧

Christmas when I was young … ah, it was grand.

PEGGY FITZGERALD

❧ 23 ❧

1834 *Last reported sighting of Great Auk in Ireland, off Waterford Harbour*
1899 *Birth of Máiréad Ní Ghráda, Irish playwright and author*
1958 *Death of Dorothy Macardle, Irish historian*

❧ 24 ❧

1946 *Departments of Health and Social Welfare established in the Republic*

Old Scotia's jocund
Highland reel
*Might make a hermit play
the deel!
So full of jig!
Famed for its* Cortillons
gay France is
But e'en give me the dance
*of dances
An Irish jig.*

LADY MORGAN

❧ YESTERDAY'S CHRISTMAS ❧

*Y*ou got your Christmas candle, always red, for nothing where you brought your groceries. And the man at the dairy across the road where we used to get our milk and butter, well, he always gave us a goose for Christmas. And everybody made Christmas pudding. Each week you'd spend a few bob and put it by until you got all the ingredients. You'd start collecting raisins and currants and the cinnamon and the nutmeg and spice. Then you'd get a big calico cloth and you'd grease it first with butter – or margarine – and then put it all in and tie it and boil that for about six or seven hours. Then leave it hanging for a few days and it would be so beautiful.

ELIZABETH 'BLUEBELL' MURPHY

⁘ 25 ⁘

Christmas Day

⁘ 26 ⁘

1916 *Birth of Kathleen O'Flaherty, Irish academic and author*

⁘ 27 ⁘

1904 *Opening of the Abbey Theatre in Dublin with a double bill,* On Baile's Strand *by W.B. Yeats and* Spreading the News *by Lady Gregory*

⁘ 28 ⁘

It is not an invitation without a drink

IRISH PROVERB

⁘ 29 ⁘

1932 *Birth of Eileen Desmond, Irish MP and Minister of Health and Social Welfare, 1981-2*

⁘ 30 ⁘

Conversation is a cure for every sorrow

TRADITIONAL SAYING

⁘ 31 ⁘

1820 *Birth of Mary Ann Sadlier, Irish novelist, businesswoman and publisher*

---

*Today shall be as
yesterday,
The red blood burns in
Ireland still.*

SUSAN MITCHELL

---

*Brief, on a flying night
From the shaken tower,
A flock of bells take flight,
And go with the hour.*

*Like birds from the cote to
the gales,
Abrupt — O hark!
A fleet of bells set sails,
And go into the dark.*

*Sudden the cold airs swing,
Alone, aloud,
A verse of bells takes wing
And flies with the cloud.*

Chimes
ALICE MEYNALL

A Symphony, John Melhuish Strudwick (1849–1937)